ORIGAMI
JEWELRY MOTIFS

ORIGAMI
JEWELRY MOTIFS

Fold and wear your own earrings,
bracelets, necklaces and more!

Julián Laboy-Rodríguez

INTERWEAVE.
interweave.com

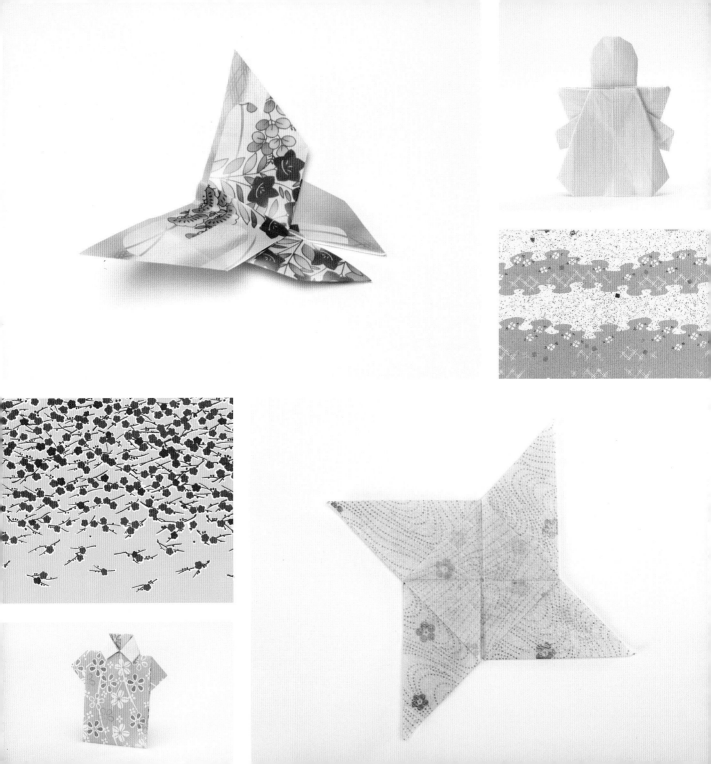

CONTENTS

INTRODUCTION

Origami has been a passion of mine since college.
I needed a simple diversion between classes, and
in origami I found both a diversion and a hobby
that I love. Since then, I have folded thousands
of models and created a few of my own. I also now
teach origami, mostly at festivals.

As with many college students, I needed extra
money to help with school and life expenses,
so I decided to sell my origami pieces. I created big
models in plastic boxes, which I sold in different
stores and markets. Experimenting with origami
jewelry was a natural next step. In December
2013, I opened an Etsy store and it has allowed
me to reach an international audience. I am proud
and happy to have met many people very interested
in the art of origami.

The projects in this book serve as an introduc-
tion to both jewelry making and origami. You will
find traditional origami models and some original
pieces, all of them accessible to jewelry making.
From simple yet elegant pieces to more complex
models, you decide the style of each piece.

Enjoy!

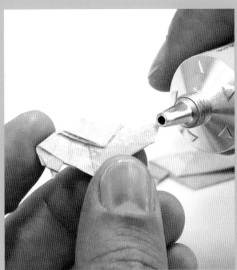

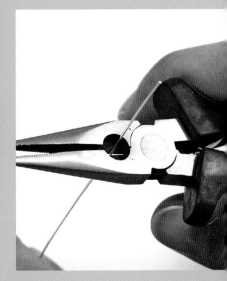

TOOLS AND MATERIALS

One of the great things about origami is that you can grab any piece of paper and start to fold. However, when creating origami models to wear and to use, special considerations are needed. The look, feel and resistance of the finished project will depend on the materials you use. Luckily there are plenty of materials to choose from, and chances are that you will easily find the ones you need at craft stores.

ORIGAMI MATERIALS

PAPER

Without paper there is no origami. But what type of paper should you use? Vibrantly colored paper can give your jewelry a flamboyant edge while more solid or serious colors denote a more elegant feel. And it's not just color you need to consider—the texture and weight of the paper must be chosen, as well.

Consider these important questions when choosing paper:

- Is it expensive? Is it hard to find?
- Does it come in the right size?
- Does it come in different colors?
- Will it tear with repeated folding?
- Will the colors fade with a protective coating or with repeated handling?
- Will it absorb the protective coating?

Let's explore a few different paper options and how they relate to these questions.

Photocopy paper

This widely available paper is a very inexpensive option. It comes in different sizes and colors, and because it's dyed in its entirety, the colors will not wear away with repeated handling or the application of a protective coating. The paper absorbs the protective coating which gives the paper more durability. However, this paper may break when used with smaller models that require repeated folding.

Magazine paper

Though the accessibility of magazines make them an appealing option, the paper is thin and may not hold up with repeated folding and the application of a protective coating. Crease marks are hard to produce. However, you can always change the paper's properties by gluing two layers of paper together. A sheet of paper with different designs on each side will create a unique look for your origami model. Don't be quick to give up on a paper. You can always do something to change its characteristics.

Origami paper

This type of paper is not hard to find. Art stores, different websites and even bookstores often carry it. It comes in many sizes, including 3" (7.6cm) squares and 10" (25.4cm) squares and has the advantage of already being a perfect square.

Origami paper is a fairly inexpensive option, especially if you purchase it in large bundles. There are many colors available, although they tend to be bright and solid. Origami paper works well with repeated folding and can absorb a protective coating for durability. However, the color may fade when coated, and if it has a color side and a white side, the white may fade first. It is a great option for practice, however.

Foil-backed paper

Foil-backed papers are an elegant option for some projects, giving the appearance of silver or gold jewelry. They're a little more difficult to find, available mostly at specialized stores and on websites. Usually, the paper comes in gold or silver on one side and white on the other.

The sizes are somewhat limited, although you may find a wider variety in wrapping paper, which is more readily available. Foil-backed paper is usually not a good candidate for a protective coating, but because of its metal component, the paper has more resistance than other types of paper. There are two varieties: Japanese and American foils.

Japanese foil is a very thin and very malleable option. That means that it can hold any shape. It's so malleable that the shape in itself may not be resistant to constant use. However, adding a second or third layer of this or another type of paper can add resistance and durability. The shiny and bright appearance is worth it!

American foil is an imitation of Japanese foil, so it has different properties. For example, the shiny surface may be a spray of color. That means the color will fade with repeated folding. The paper tends to be spongy and thick, so it doesn't hold shapes as easily as Japanese foil. It is a less expensive version of foil paper, so it may be a good option for very simple models.

Washi

In general, washi (which literally means "Japanese paper") is the best option for the pieces included in this book. The only drawback is the price: This paper is more expensive than the others and it is not readily available.

The arrangement of the paper fibers makes this paper strong, and it is made even stronger and more durable when the protective coating is added.

Washi paper doesn't break with more than usual stress; it comes in various colors and wonderful patterns as well as soft, fabric-like textures; and it folds beautifully with small and large models. Washi paper includes a wide variety of papers—I encourage you to experiment with them to find the ones you like best.

CUTTING

Depending on the type of paper you choose, you may need to cut your paper to size before beginning to fold. Origami is a precise craft, so it's important to take care when measuring and cutting your paper. These tools will help you:

Scissors

Chances are you already have a pair of scissors on hand. Since most of the jewelry projects in this book are small, a small pair of scissors with short, sharp blades is ideal. You may also use scissors with larger blades for bigger pieces of paper. Make sure your scissors are sharp!

Craft knife

A craft knife is a great option for cutting a straight, precise line. Be sure to place a cutting mat underneath the paper to protect your work surface. Use a safety ruler to guide the blade.

Paper trimmer

Paper trimmers offer a very safe, fast and accurate way to cut paper, thanks to a rotary blade and a sliding shuttle.

FOLDING

Precise, crisp folds are critical to producing professional-looking origami models.

Bone or plastic folder

Use these to press on freshly glued surfaces and to fold the paper crisply and firmly. You could use your fingernails, but a bone or plastic folder will keep your hands clean and free from glue.

Toothpick

Sometimes your fingernails aren't enough. When folding and trying to reach small spaces, this tool will come in handy. You can also use it later to glue small areas.

GLUING

There are times when you'll need glue to finish your origami models. Or, you may want to glue sheets of paper together before you begin folding. Choose a glue that will dry clear and strong.

Uhu All Purpose Adhesive is a very good option for gluing paper to paper. It doesn't fully set for two to three minutes, so you have some time to rearrange the paper if needed. This glue is not suitable for gluing paper to metal. It is inexpensive and can be found at most craft stores.

Other options include Elmer's Carpenter's Wood Glue and LePage White Glue. Both take longer to dry than Uhu glue. In some projects, such as the hair pins, you'll need to use a metal glue to adhere the paper to the metal base of the pin. I recommend JB Weld. E6000 is good for attaching end caps to cording.

COATING

Adding a protective coating to your finished origami model can give the model structure, and depending on what you use, can provide a glossy finish and make the model somewhat water repellent.

Water

If you don't like working with certain chemicals, you can spray water onto the finished origami model instead. When dry, the model will hold its shape better and will be stiffer and more durable.

However, spraying the model with water will not provide protection from rain and sunlight. When damp, the paper will lose its shape slightly; be sure to reshape the model as needed before the paper dries completely.

Crystal clear acrylic coating

This coating comes in an easy-to-use spray can, and it has a permanent protective gloss finish that prevents paper from yellowing with age. It is moisture resistant and dries in minutes. Be sure to spray on a nonstick surface such as wax paper and follow the manufacturer's directions.

Kamar varnish

This varnish has the same advantages of the crystal clear acrylic coating but makes paper even more durable, highly resistant to discoloration and strong. This varnish is a favorite of mine. Again, be sure to spray on a nonstick surface such as wax paper and follow the manufacturer's directions.

Satin-finish water-based polyurethane

This finish can be tricky to work with and won't hold up well to heat and certain chemicals, but it will harden your paper while perserving some of the paper's flexibility.

JEWELRY TOOLS & MATERIALS

TOOLS

The jewelry projects in this book aren't overly complicated, but they do require a few special tools and supplies to make. I recommend that you have chain-nose pliers on hand, which are good for opening and closing jewelry findings. Round-nose pliers are helpful for bending and pinching pins and wire. You'll also need a pair of flush cutters to cut your chain and findings. Look for tools made of stainless steel, which won't mar your origami models.

FINDINGS

The projects in this book range from earrings to necklaces to bracelets and more. You'll need different findings to make the various pieces, but they should all be pretty easy to obtain.

Earring findings

The projects in this book use both fishhook earrings and post earrings with a blank. You have options when it comes to making earrings—the findings come in different colors, types of metal and gauge. I usually use hypoallergenic materials such as stainless steel, surgical steel or silver. Your project may call for a specific type of earring finding, but feel free to experiment with other types.

Headpins and eye pins

Headpins and eye pins are useful for making and attaching origami charms. Craft wire can also be used as a substitute.

Pin backs

There are a few different styles when it comes to pin backs—choose the style that appeals to you, as long as it has a blank surface to which your origami model can be attached.

Hairpins

Look for a hairpin with a blank, which is essentially a bobby pin with a disk for gluing on an attachment. They come in a variety of finishes and sizes.

Headbands

Choose a thin headband with a ribbon finish that coordinates with your origami model.

Rings

Look for an adjustable ring with a blank base. The ring will fit a wide range of sizes and have a base for attaching your model.

Cording

Cording comes in a variety of materials such as silk and leather. It makes a great option for bracelets and necklaces. You'll need cord ends to attach clasps to your cord. Make sure you buy the size appropriate for your cord.

Clasps

You have many choices when it comes to your clasp: lobster and S-hooks are the clasps I use most often. You can buy them in any finish and a variety of sizes.

Small cable chain

Chain is available in different sizes, styles and thicknesses. As with earring supplies, you can use hypoallergenic materials or good quality silver and gold. A standard length for necklaces is 18" (45.7cm).

Premade options

When buying materials for bracelets and necklaces, there are a number of premade options you can use. A necklace with a clasp already attached works well for charms anchored to the chain, and premade bracelets are available with removable clasps, so you can slide your charms and beads on, then replace the clasp.

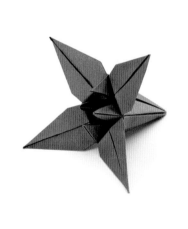

ORIGAMI MODELS

This part of the book will teach you how to fold the models (origami figures) used in the jewelry projects. Each model gives you a recommended paper size (though you can experiment with different sizes) and a difficulty level. None of the models in this book are terribly complex—the most difficult folds are appropriate for the intermediate level.

Look over what each of the symbols means before you start folding, and always work on a clean flat surface. I suggest starting with the easier models just to get the hang of folding with such small paper. Once you're finished folding, follow the instructions at the beginning of the Jewelry Projects chapter for preparing the models.

ORIGAMI BASICS

SYMBOLS

These symbols are used almost universally in the paper-folding community, so they will come in handy for our projects and beyond. Make yourself familiar with these symbols before practicing some of the basic folds.

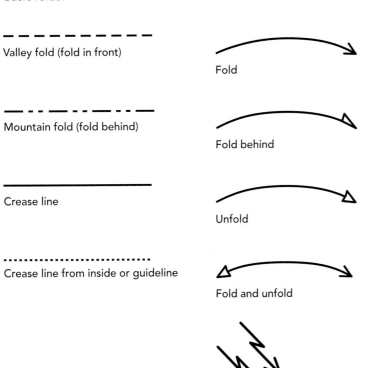

Valley fold (fold in front)

Mountain fold (fold behind)

Crease line

Crease line from inside or guideline

Fold

Fold behind

Unfold

Fold and unfold

Crimp fold (valley-fold on the front and back)

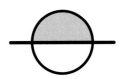

Paper right side (color side) up

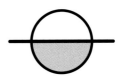

Paper wrong side (white side) up

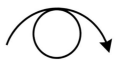

Turn over

Open   Push or press

Repeat step where marked. The number of dashes on the arrow indicates the number of repeats.

Fold/tuck inside

BASIC FOLDS

Many of these folds are used for the foundation of the models. Rather than walk you through the steps each time, you'll see an illustration in the model instructions that requires the series of folds shown here.

Inside-Reverse Fold

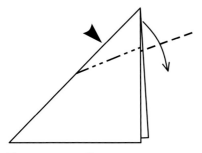

The step as you'll see it throughout the book.

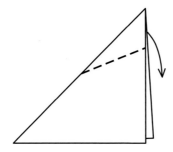

1 Valley-fold down.

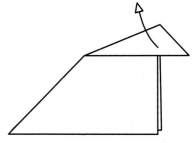

2 Unfold.

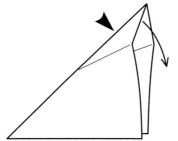

3 Fold down, pushing between the layers.

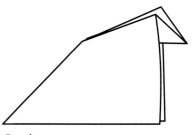

Result

Outside-Reverse Fold

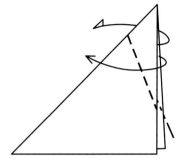

The step as you'll see
it throughout the book.

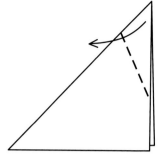

1 Valley-fold to the left.

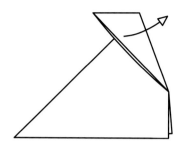

2 Unfold.

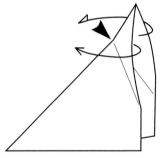

3 Open and flip the corner over.

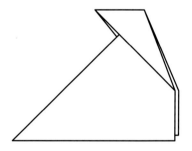

Result

Preliminary Base

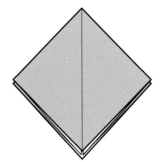

The step as you'll see
it throughout the book.

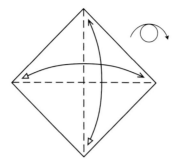

1 Valley-fold and unfold. Turn over.

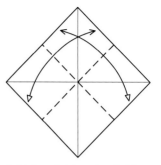

2 Valley-fold and unfold.

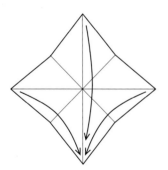

3 Collapse along the previous folds.

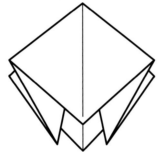

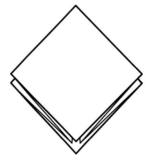

Result

Water Bomb Base

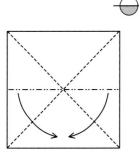

The step as you'll see
it throughout the book.

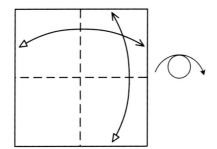

1 Fold and unfold. Turn over.

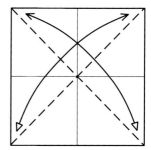

2 Fold and unfold.

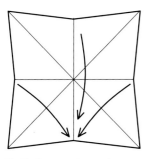
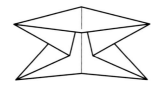

3 Collapse along the previous folds.

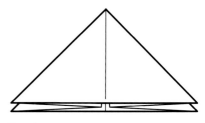

Result

Squash Fold

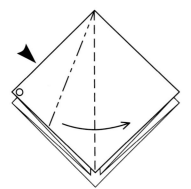

The step as you'll see it throughout the book.

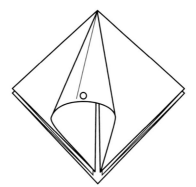

1 Fold to the right while opening the flap to the left. Flatten.

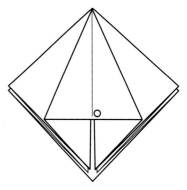

Result

FOLDING TIPS

- Familiarize yourself with the symbols. Each one is important.
- Whenever possible, fold on a clean, flat surface. It will make your folds more precise.
- Make sharp, crisp folds using bone or plastic folders. Crisp folds help you define each step and may make subsequent folds easier, but they will also give your models a flat finish.
- If creating a more 3-D model, make less defined folds in the final steps. This will give your model a more rounded look after applying the coating.

- Look to the next step to see how your model should look when you complete the current step.
- Precision is important, especially in projects with many steps. Fold carefully!
- Work slowly and carefully, especially with small paper.
- If you're having trouble with a step, take a break. Often coming back with a clear head is the best remedy.
- Be especially careful when folding metallic papers. Crisp folds are permanent with them.

HEART

SKILL LEVEL
★ ★ ☆

PAPER SIZE
1½" (3.8cm) for smaller models

SUGGESTED PROJECTS
Good for all projects

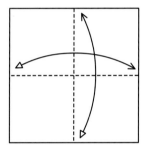

1 Valley-fold and unfold.

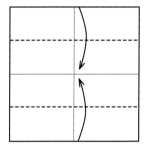

2 Valley-fold.

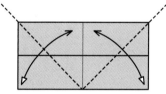

3 Valley-fold and unfold. The 2 corners will meet at the top.

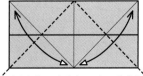

4 Valley-fold and unfold. The 2 corners will meet at the bottom.

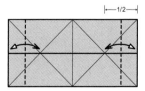

5 Valley-fold and unfold.

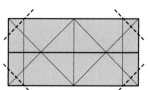

6 Valley-fold the corners so that they meet with the folds from step 5.

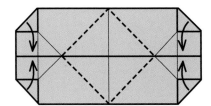

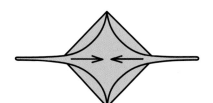

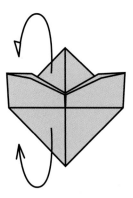

7 Pinch the left and right sides while making a valley fold. The model will not lie flat.

8 View from above of finished step 7.

9 Fold both flaps down, bringing the points together at the bottom.

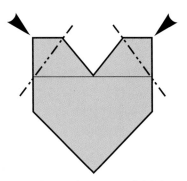

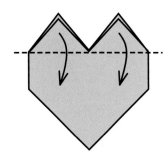

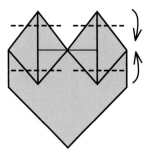

10 Inside-reverse-fold the 2 top corners.

11 Valley-fold down the top layer of the tips.

12 Valley-fold the 4 tips.

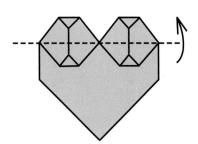

13 Valley-fold the top back up.

Result

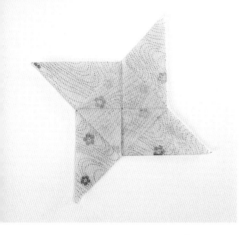

FOUR-POINTED STAR

SKILL LEVEL
★ ☆ ☆

PAPER SIZE
1½" (3.8cm)

SUGGESTED PROJECTS
Good for all projects

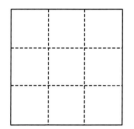

1 With the wrong side of the paper facing you, valley-fold in thirds.

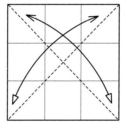

2 Valley-fold and unfold.

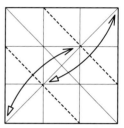

3 Valley-fold and unfold.

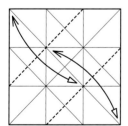

4 Valley-fold and unfold.

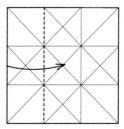

5 Valley-fold to the right.

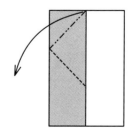

6 Pinch the corner of the top layer with a mountain fold and valley-fold down. The model will not lie flat.

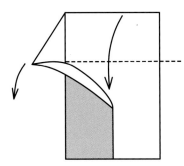

7 Valley-fold across the folds in step 6. This will flatten the model.

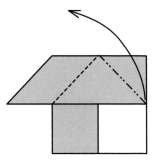

8 Repeat steps 6 and 7 on the top portion of the model.

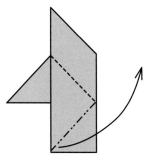

9 Repeat steps 6 and 7 on what is now the right side of the model.

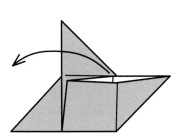

10 Pull the corner trapped in the middle to the outside.

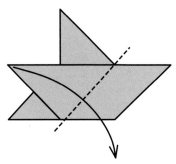

11 Valley-fold that corner down.

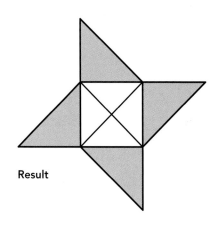

Result

SAILBOAT

SKILL LEVEL
★ ★ ★

PAPER SIZE
1½" (3.8cm) for small models

SUGGESTED PROJECTS
Good for all projects

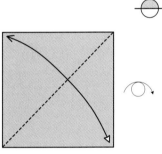

1 With the paper right side up, valley-fold and unfold. Turn the model over.

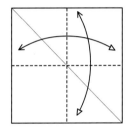

2 Valley-fold and unfold.

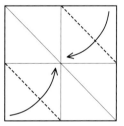

3 Valley-fold 2 corners.

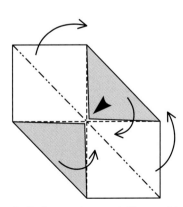

4 Collapse the model by pushing gently in the middle and following the crease lines.

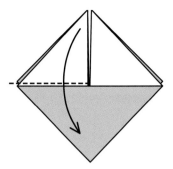

5 Valley-fold the left sail down.

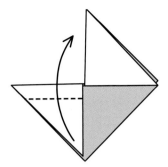

6 Valley-fold the sail back up.

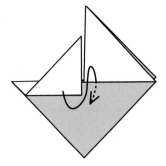

7 Hide the excess paper below the middle line by opening the pocket in the middle and tucking the paper inside.

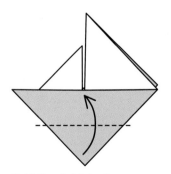

8 Valley-fold the bottom up, so that the bottom point touches the middle. Turn the model over.

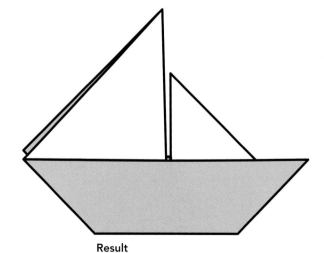

Result

SHIRT

SKILL LEVEL
★ ★ ☆

PAPER SIZE
2" (5.1cm) for small models

SUGGESTED PROJECTS
Good for all projects

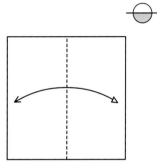

1 With the paper wrong side up, valley-fold and unfold. Cut the paper along the fold. You need only 1 rectangle for this model.

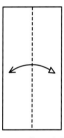

2 Valley-fold and unfold.

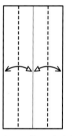

3 Valley-fold and unfold each side.

4 Mountain-fold the top edge. Valley-fold the bottom corners so that they meet the closest crease.

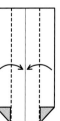

5 Valley-fold each side.

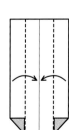

6 Mountain-fold the top. Fold and unfold the bottom.

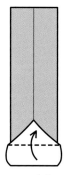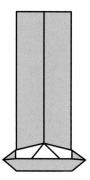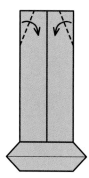

7 Open the bottom while performing a valley fold. Continue pushing until the bottom lies flat.

8 Valley-fold the top corners down. This will form the collar.

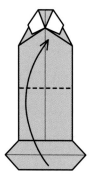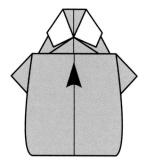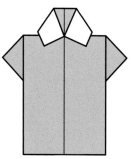

9 Valley-fold the bottom up so that the bottom edge is even with the outer edges of the collar.

10 Tuck the bottom edge under the collar points. Flatten the model.

Result

PURSE

SKILL LEVEL
★ ☆ ☆

PAPER SIZE
1½" (3.8cm) for small models

SUGGESTED PROJECTS
Dangle earrings, necklaces. Be careful with
the purse handle; it is delicate.

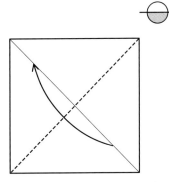

1 With the paper wrong side up,
valley-fold it in half.

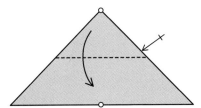

2 Rotate the paper so that the
fold is along the bottom.
Valley-fold the top layer down.
Repeat with the bottom layer.

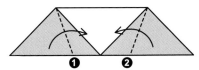

3 Valley-fold on the left first,
then the right.

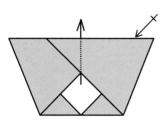

4 Pull the trapped layer out from behind the flaps. Pull the back layer up as well.

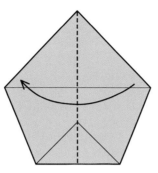

5 Valley-fold the model in half.

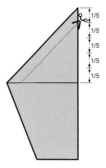

1/5
1/5
1/5
1/5
1/5

6 Cut the paper half way down, about one-fifth from the edge, as indicated.

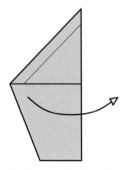

7 Unfold the fold from step 5.

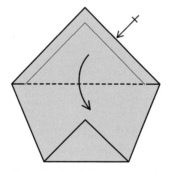

8 Valley-fold the top flap down. Repeat on the back side.

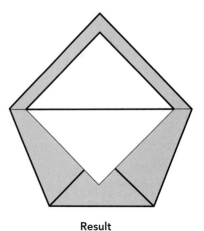

Result

SAMURAI HELMET

SKILL LEVEL
★ ★ ★

PAPER SIZE
1½" (3.8cm) for small models

SUGGESTED PROJECTS
Dangle earrings, necklaces. Because of the pocket created during the folding, it's a good choice for post earrings, as well.

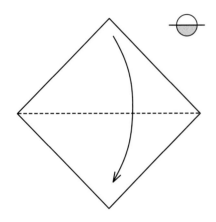

1 With the paper wrongside up, valley-fold it in half.

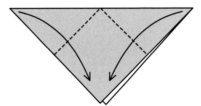

2 Valley-fold down the corners.

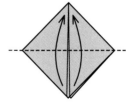

3 Valley-fold up the top layers.

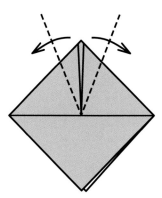

4 Valley-fold the top points.

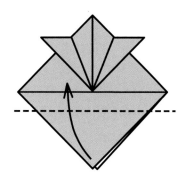

5 Valley-fold up the top layer.

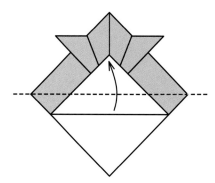

6 Valley-fold up the top layer.

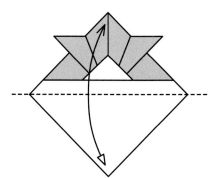

7 Valley-fold up the back layer, then unfold.

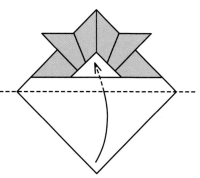

8 Tuck the back layer into the pocket with a valley fold. Alternatively, mountain-fold the back layer.

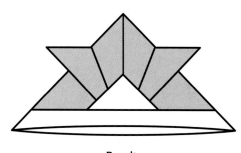

Result

GOLDFISH

SKILL LEVEL
★ ★ ★

PAPER SIZE
1½" (3.8cm) for small models

SUGGESTED PROJECTS
Good for all projects

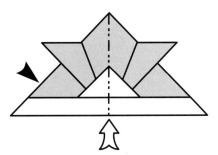

1 Begin with a finished Samurai Helmet. Open the model by pushing on the sides and flattening them.

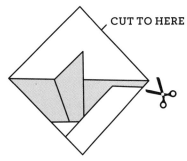

CUT TO HERE

2 Cut the top layer until you reach the line indicated. Rotate the model to the right.

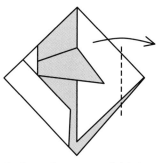

3 Outside-reverse-fold the tail to the right.

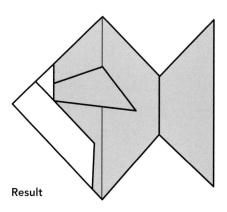

Result

BUTTERFLY

SKILL LEVEL
★ ☆ ☆

PAPER SIZE
  1½" (3.8cm) for small models

SUGGESTED PROJECTS
  Good for all projects because of flat back

TIP

The tips of the wings on this butterfly can be fragile. If you're making butterflies to use with jewlery, choose a stronger paper so that the tips don't bend with use.

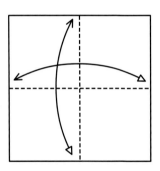

1 With the paper wrong side up, valley-fold and unfold.

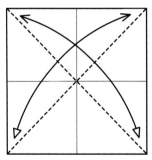

2 Again, valley-fold and unfold.

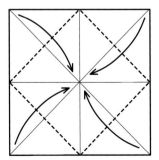

3 Valley-fold down each corner so that they meet in the center.

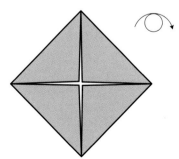

4 Turn the model over.

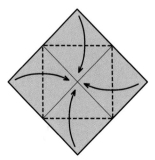

5 Valley-fold the corners down again so that they meet at the center.

6 At the end of step 5, your model should look like this.

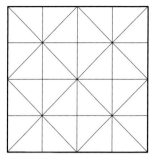

7 Unfold everything. Your model should look like this.

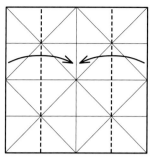

8 Valley-fold opposite sides to meet at the center.

9 Valley-fold the upper layers. You'll need to open the model. It will not lie flat until step 11.

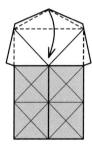

10 Continue valley-folding down to flatten the model.

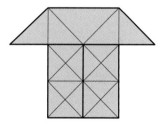

11 This is what your model should look like at the end of step 10. Rotate the model 180°.

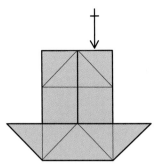

12 Repeat steps 10 and 11 on the top half of the model.

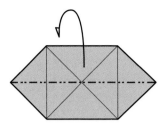
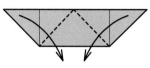

13 Mountain-fold the model in half.

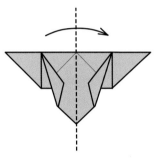

14 Valley-fold down the top tips.

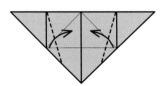

15 Valley-fold toward the center.

16 Valley-fold the model in half.

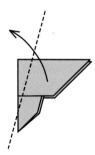

17 Valley-fold the top layer only to form a set of wings.

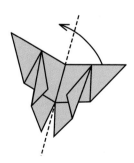

18 Repeat step 17 on the other half. It's easier to align the wings if you fold them one at a time.

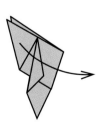

19 Open the wings. The model will not lie flat in the middle.

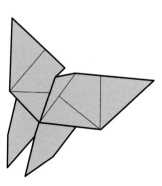

Result

TURTLE

SKILL LEVEL
★ ★ ☆

PAPER SIZE
1¼"–1½" (3.2cm–3.8cm) for small models

SUGGESTED PROJECTS
Good for all projects

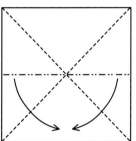

1 With the paper wrong side up, collapse the paper to form a water bomb base.

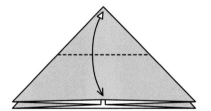

2 Valley-fold and unfold to create a crease for the next step.

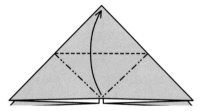

3 Valley-fold the top layer up, incorporating 2 mountain folds as indicated.

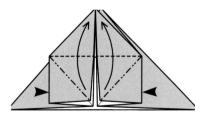

4 Fold the tips to the top.

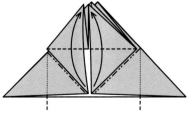

5 Keep folding up as in step 2, but incorporate valley folds into both sides.

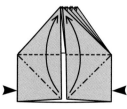

6 Fold the tips to the top as you did in step 3.

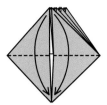

7 Valley-fold down the 2 front tips.

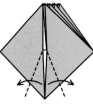

8 Valley-fold the bottom tips as indicated. These will be the rear fins.

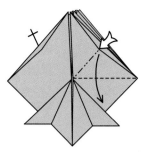

9 Perform a squash fold on the right side, then on the left.

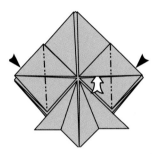

10 Perform another set of squash folds on both sides.

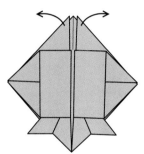

11 Slide the tips away from the center, but not all the way. Press the new folds.

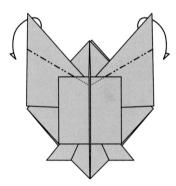

12 Mountain-fold the tips to the back.

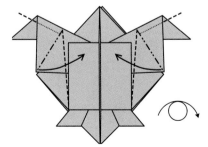

13 Valley-fold part of the right side toward the center, incorporating a mountain fold and pressing on the excess. Repeat on the left side, then turn the model over.

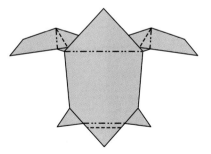

14 Mountain-fold the middle front tip, hiding it in a pocket. Shape the front fins. Mountain- and valley-fold the bottom to shape the tail.

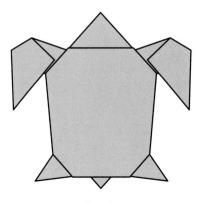

Result

SITTING DOG

SKILL LEVEL
★ ☆ ☆

PAPER SIZE
1½" (3.8cm) for small models

SUGGESTED PROJECTS
The pocket in the middle makes this perfect for post earrings, but it works well for all projects.

1 With the paper wrong side up, fold it and unfold it in half.

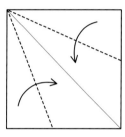

2 Fold the edges to the center.

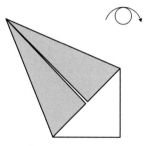

3 After step 2, the model will look like this. Turn it over.

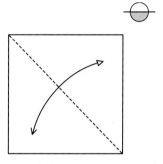

4 Valley-fold down in half.

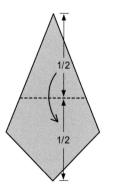

5 Valley-fold the front flap almost to the edge of the model.

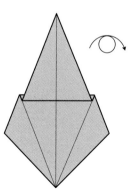

6 After step 5, the model will look like this. Turn it over.

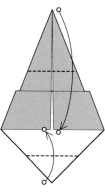

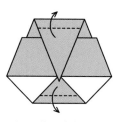

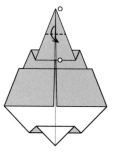

7 Valley-fold the top and bottom until the respective dots meet.

8 Valley-fold the top and bottom flaps.

9 Valley fold the top in half.

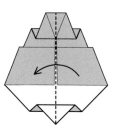

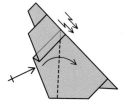

10 Valley-fold the entire model in half.

11 After step 10, the model should look like this. Rotate it slightly to the left.

12 Make a valley-fold on the front and back. This makes a crimp fold that forms the front legs and pulls the head down, differentiating the head from the rest of the body.

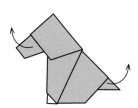

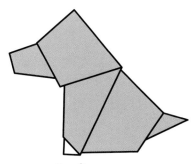

13 Slide the nose and tail slightly as indicated.

Result

ELEPHANT

SKILL LEVEL
★ ★ ☆

PAPER SIZE
1½" (3.8cm) for small models

SUGGESTED PROJECTS
The pocket in the middle makes this perfect for post earrings, but it works well for all projects.

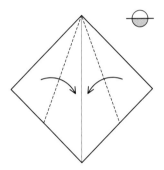

1 With the paper wrong side up, valley-fold the edges to the middle.

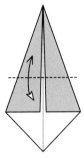

2 Valley-fold in half and unfold.

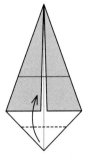

3 Valley-fold up the bottom tip. This will form the tail.

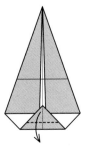

4 Valley-fold down. This will continue to shape the tail.

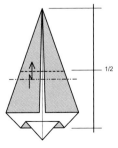

5 Fold mountain and valley folds as indicated.

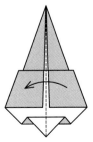

6 Valley-fold the entire model in half.

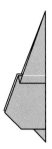 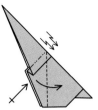 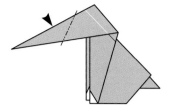

7 After step 6, the model will look like this. Roate it slightly to the left.

8 Fold a valley and mountain fold on the front, then repeat on the back.

9 Inside-reverse-fold to form the trunk.

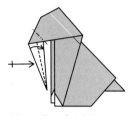 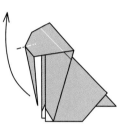 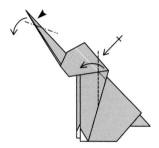

10 Valley-fold the trunk in half as indicated, and mountain-fold the excess. Repeat behind.

11 Move the trunk upwards with an inside-reverse fold. The position of the trunk can be altered to your preference.

12 Inside-reverse-fold to finish the trunk. Valley-fold to form an ear. Repeat behind to finish the other ear.

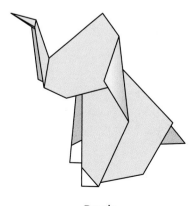

Result

FOX

SKILL LEVEL
★ ☆ ☆

PAPER SIZE
1½" (3.8cm) for small models

SUGGESTED PROJECTS
The pocket in the middle makes this perfect for post earrings.
The flat back is perfect for brooches, rings and headbands.

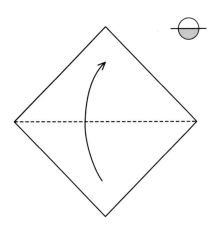

1 With the paper wrong side up, valley-fold in half.

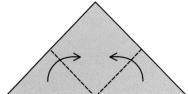

2 Valley-fold both corners to meet in the middle.

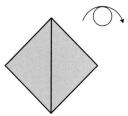

3 After step 2, the model will look like this. Turn it over.

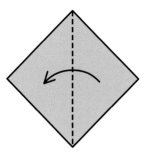

4 Valley-fold in half.

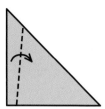

5 Rotate the model to the left and valley-fold all layers. This will give shape to the front legs and head.

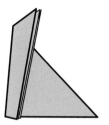

6 After step 5, the model will look like this.

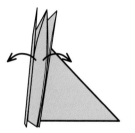

7 Open as indicated. The model will not lie flat at this point.

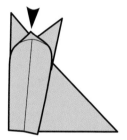

8 Squash fold the middle layer to give shape to the head.

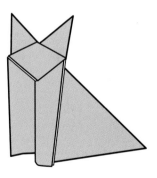

Result

CRANE

SKILL LEVEL
★ ★ ☆

PAPER SIZE
1½" (3.8cm) for small models

SUGGESTED PROJECTS
This 3-D model works best with dangle earrings and bracelets.

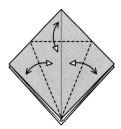

1 Begin with a preliminary base.

2 Valley-fold and unfold as indicated.

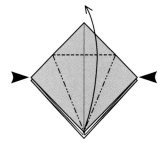

3 Valley-fold up the top flap and squash-fold using the creases created in step 2.

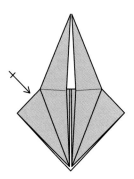

4 Repeat steps 2 and 3 on the back.

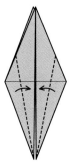

5 Fold 2 valley folds so that the bottom edges meet in the center.

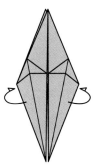

6 Repeat step 5 on the back.

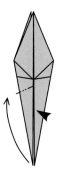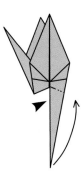

7 Inside-reverse-fold on the left side.

8 Inside-reverse-fold on the right side.

9 Inside-reverse-fold to form the head.

10 Pull the flaps down to form the wings.

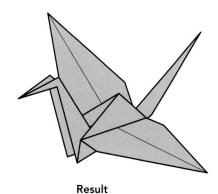

Result

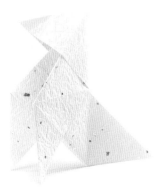

PAJARITA

SKILL LEVEL
★ ★ ☆

PAPER SIZE
1½" (3.8cm) for small models

SUGGESTED PROJECTS
Works wells for dangle earrings, bracelets and necklaces.

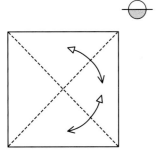

1 With the paper wrong side up, valley-fold and unfold.

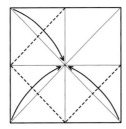

2 Valley-fold 3 corners to the center.

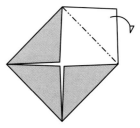

3 Moutain-fold the remaining corner to the back.

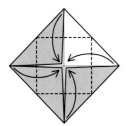

4 Valley-fold all 4 corners to the middle.

5 After step 4, the model will look like this. Turn it over.

6 Valley-fold in half.

7 Open the middle slightly and pull out the 2 corners trapped in the middle.

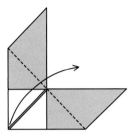

8 Valley-fold up the front flap.

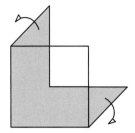

9 Fold the 2 corner flaps to the back.

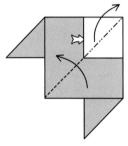

10 Valley-fold the model in half while mountain-folding the top to create the head.

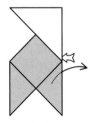

11 Slide out a trapped corner to create the tail.

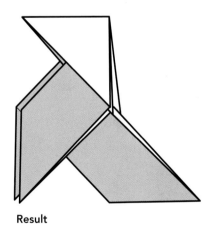

Result

OWL

SKILL LEVEL
★ ☆ ☆

PAPER SIZE
1½" (3.8cm) for small models

SUGGESTED PROJECTS
When left flat, this model is good for post earrings, brooches and rings.

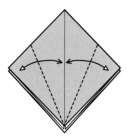

1 Begin with a preliminary base. Valley-fold and unfold the sides.

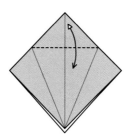

2 Valley-fold and unfold the top.

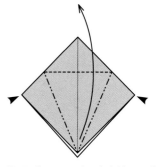

3 Following the fold lines from the previous step, pull the top layer up and flatten it with a squash fold.

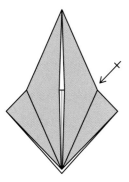

4 Repeat on the other side.

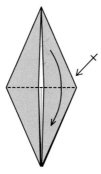

5 Valley-fold the front flap down. Repeat on the back.

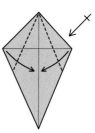

6 Valley-fold the corners to the center. Repeat on the back.

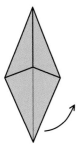
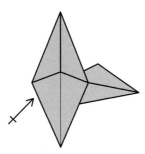
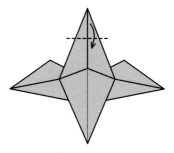

7 Slide the interior flap to the middle so that it creates a wing.

8 Repeat the previous step on the left side.

9 Valley-fold down the upper tip.

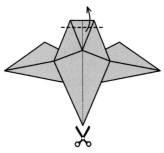
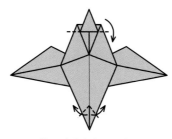
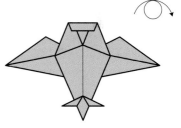

10 Valley-fold the tip up, then cut the bottom as shown.

11 Valley-fold down the top. Valley-fold the bottom to form legs.

12 After step 11, the model will look like this. Turn the model over.

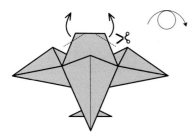
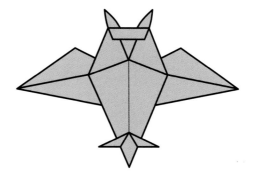

13 Cut the top layer and pull the paper up to create ears. Turn over.

Result

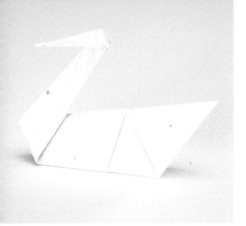

SWAN

SKILL LEVEL
★ ★ ★

PAPER SIZE
1½" (3.8cm) for small models

SUGGESTED PROJECTS
This model works well as a charm. Take care when balancing the charm.

TIP

Both sides of the paper show quite a bit on this model. Keep that in mind when choosing your paper. Look for something that is similarly colored on both sides or that has complimentary colors on either side. If you can't find something you like, consider gluing two pieces of paper together to create the perfect paper.

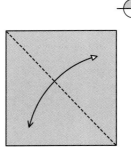

1 With the paper right side up, valley-fold and unfold.

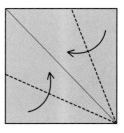

2 Valley-fold to the center.

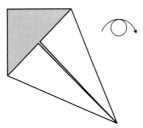

3 After step 2, the model will look like this. Turn it over.

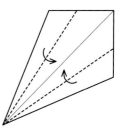

4 Valley-fold to the center.

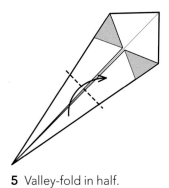

5 Valley-fold in half.

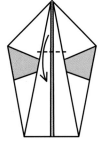

6 Valley-fold down the tip.

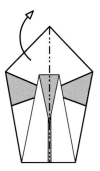

7 Valley-fold the entire model in half.

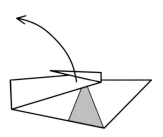

8 Slide up the neck.

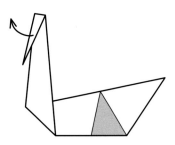

9 Slide up the head.

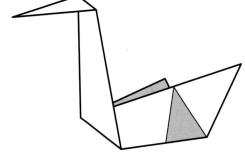

Result

JAPANESE MAN

SKILL LEVEL
★ ★ ★

PAPER SIZE
1½" (3.8cm) for small models

SUGGESTED PROJECTS
This flat model works well with all jewelry types.

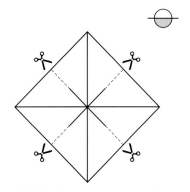

1 With the paper wrong side up, cut as indicated.

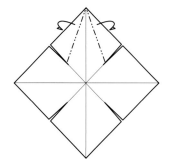

2 Mountain-fold to the back.

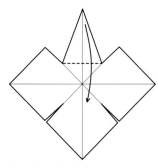

3 Valley-fold the tip down.

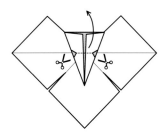

4 Cut small triangles from the left and right sides of the tip at the midline. Unfold the tip.

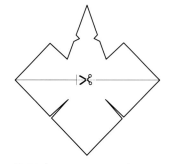

5 Make a tiny cut in the middle of the paper to create a pocket.

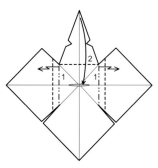

6 Crimp-fold (mountain-fold, then valley-fold) on the right and left sides. Valley-fold down the tip and hide it in the middle cut from the previous step.

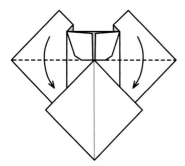

7 Valley-fold down.

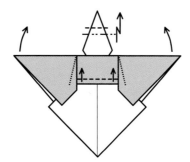

8 Crimp-fold the tip of the head to shape it. Slide the arms slightly toward the top. Valley-fold a thin layer in the middle.

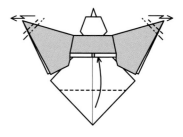

9 Crimp-fold the tip of each arm to give it some shape. Valley-fold the bottom, hiding the tip as indicated.

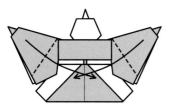

10 Valley-fold down the arms.

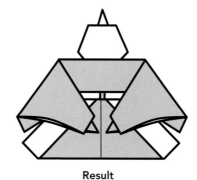

Result

FRACTAL ROSE

SKILL LEVEL
★ ☆ ☆

PAPER SIZE
2" (5.1cm) for small models

SUGGESTED PROJECTS
This model works well for all jewelry projects. The back is flat, but the petals give it a 3-D effect.

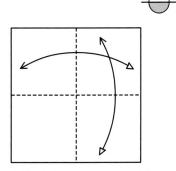

1 With the paper right side up, vally-fold and unfold.

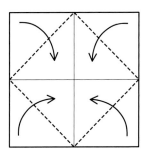

2 Valley-fold all 4 corners to the center.

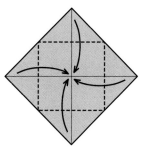

3 Valley-fold the corners to the center again.

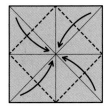

4 Valley-fold the corners to the center for a third time.

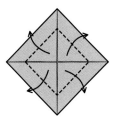

5 Unfold the center tips.

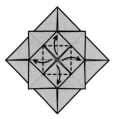

6 Valley-fold the 4 corners in the center.

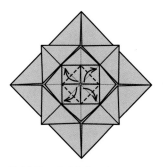 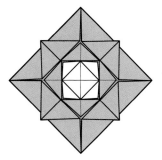 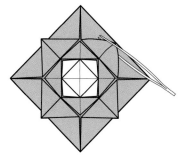

7 Valley-fold the 4 new corners in the center.

8 After step 7, the model will look like this.

9 Gently bend the petals back with your fingers or tweezers to give the rose a full, rounded look.

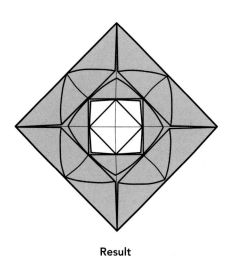

Result

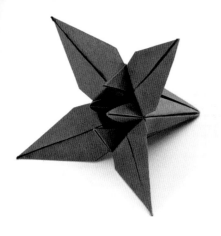

LILY

SKILL LEVEL
★★☆

PAPER SIZE
1¾" (4.4cm) for small models

SUGGESTED PROJECTS
This model works well for bracelets, necklaces and dangle earrings.

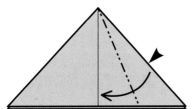

1 Begin with a water bomb base. Make a squash fold in the upper right flap.

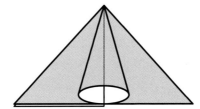

2 During step 1, the model will look like this.

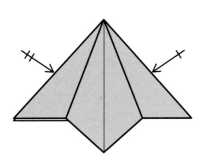

3 Repeat step 1 once on the right and two times on the left.

RESULT

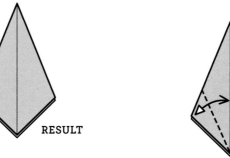

4 Fold to the center and unfold.

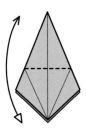

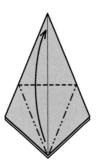

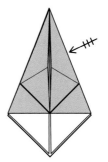

5 Valley-fold and unfold the upper layer.

6 Valley-fold up a petal.

7 Repeat steps 4–6 on the other 3 sides.

RESULT

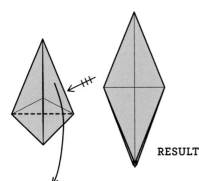

RESULT

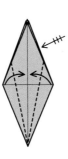

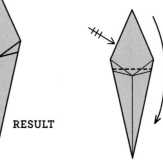

RESULT

8 Valley-fold down and repeat on the other 3 sides. Rotate the model 180°.

9 Valley-fold to the center. Repeat on the other 3 sides.

10 Valley-fold the petals down. Repeat on the other 3 petals.

TIP

Curve the petals with subtle moutain folds, or bend them over a thin, round object, such as a pencil.

STOCKING

SKILL LEVEL
★ ★ ☆

PAPER SIZE
1½" (3.8cm) for small models

SUGGESTED PROJECTS
This model works well with all styles of jewelry, especially the post earrings.

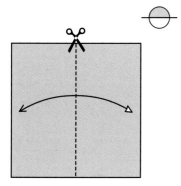

1 With the paper right side up, fold and cut the paper down the middle. Set one rectangle aside to use for something else.

2 Valley-fold down the top edge.

3 After step 2, the model will look like this. Turn it over.

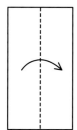

4 Valley-fold in half.

5 Valley-fold in half.

6 Valley-fold down the front flap as indicated.

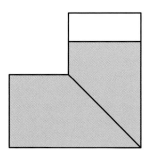

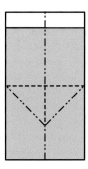

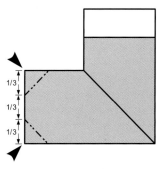

7 Completed step 6. Unfold the model back to step 3.

8 Refold the model with the new valley and mountain folds shown. Sink and hide the middle with the new folds.

9 Inside-reverse-fold the 2 corners of the toe.

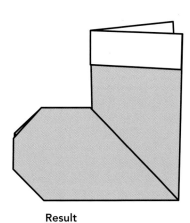

Result

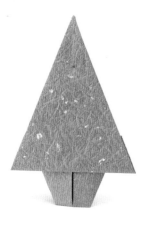

CHRISTMAS TREE

SKILL LEVEL
★ ☆ ☆

PAPER SIZE
1" (2.5cm) for small models

SUGGESTED PROJECTS
This model works well with all styles of jewelry and can be made very small.

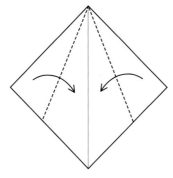

1 With the paper wrong-side up, valley-fold the paper in half and unfold.

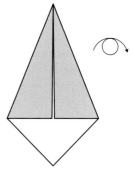

2 Valley-fold each side so the edges meet at the middle.

3 After step 2, the model will look lik this. Turn it over.

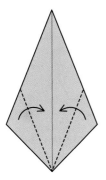

4 Valley-fold each bottom side so the edges meet at the middle.

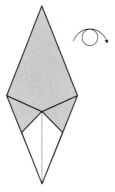

5 After step 4, the model will look like this. Turn it over.

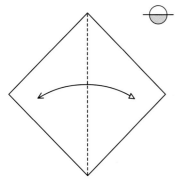

6 Valley-fold in half.

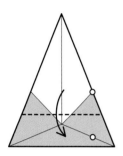

7 Valley-fold the front, aligning the points shown.

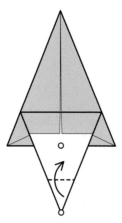

8 Valley-fold up the bottom tip, aligning the points as shown. This is the trunk of the tree.

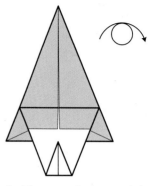

9 After step 8, the model will look like this. Turn it over.

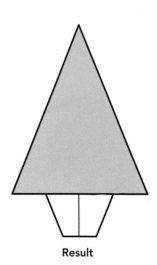

Result

FISH

SKILL LEVEL
★ ★ ☆

PAPER SIZE
1¾" (4.4cm) for small models

SUGGESTED PROJECTS
This model works well with dangle earrings

TIP

This model is meant to be three-dimensional. Play with the side fins until they jut out at just the right angle.

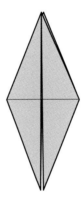

1 Fold steps 1 through 4 of the Crane (NOT the Flat Crane).

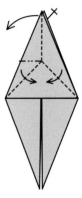

2 Fold the valley and mountain folds as indicated. Repeat behind. The tips should point in the same direction.

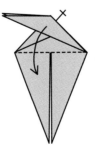

3 Valley-fold down. Repeat behind.

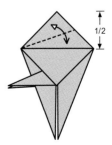

4 Fold the top portion in half and then unfold it.

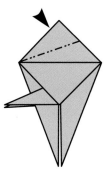

5 Sink the previous fold to the inside by opening the top and folding a moutain-fold along the line created in the previous step (see Tip).

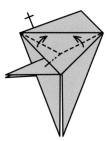

6 Valley- and mountain-fold to the inside. The fin will turn over. Repeat behind.

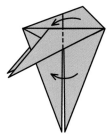

7 Valley-fold the top layer to the left.

TIP

Step 5 is a difficult step. You'll need to open the top of the model almost completely and fold the line bit by bit. After making the inside fold, you'll need to reshape the model. It's almost as if you are folding a double inside-reverse fold, but since you're working with one piece, it ends up being one big fold.

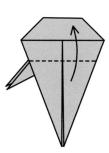

8 Valley-fold up the top layer.

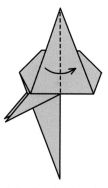

9 Valley-fold to the right.

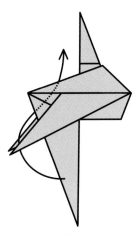

10 Valley-fold the tip up until it stops.

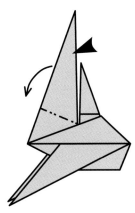

11 Inside-reverse-fold as indicated.

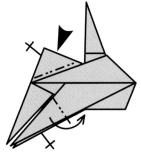

12 Fold an inside-reverse fold on the top and another on the bottom. Repeat behind.

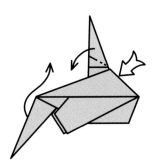

13 Outside-reverse-fold the top fin, and fold the left fin to the top.

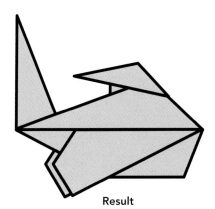

Result

LADYBUG

SKILL LEVEL
★★☆

PAPER SIZE
2" (5.1cm) for small models

SUGGESTED PROJECTS
The ladybug is hard to make small, so use it for projects that need bigger models, such as necklaces, brooches or hairpins.

TIP

The dots on the ladybug can be tricky to fold in small sizes. Using a toothpick or a needle will help you fold them.

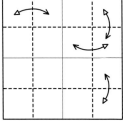

1 With the paper wrong side up, valley-fold and unfold as indicated.

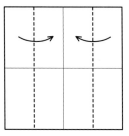

2 Fold 2 valley folds.

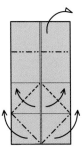

3 Mountain-fold the top half to the back. Fold valley and mountain folds in the bottom half as indicated.

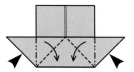

4 Squash-fold the 2 squares in the bottom.

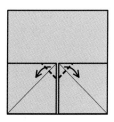

5 Valley-fold the tips. These will be the ladybug's dots.

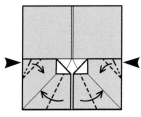

6 Squash-fold the top outer corners of the bottom squares. Valley-fold each bottom square.

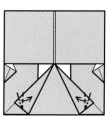

7 Squash-fold the bottom tips.

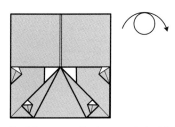

8 After step 7, the model will look like this. Turn it over.

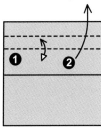

9 Valley-fold the top in half and unfold. Valley-fold the the top half in half.

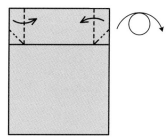

10 Squash-fold on the left and right sides as indicated. Turn the paper over.

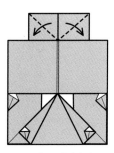

11 Valley-fold down on the left and right. The flaps will go into the pocket between the head and the body.

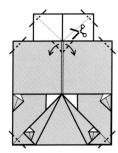

12 Mountain-fold the tips to the back as indicated to shape the model. Cut just under the head to the left and right, and valley-fold the newly formed tips to create one last set of dots.

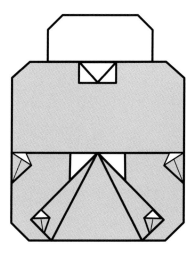

Result

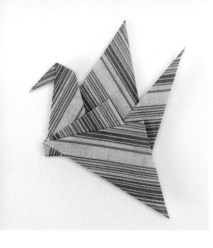

FLAT CRANE

SKILL LEVEL
★ ★ ☆

PAPER SIZE
1½" (3.8cm) for small models

SUGGESTED PROJECTS
The opening between the body and back wing makes this perfect for post earrings. The flat back works well for brooches, rings and headbands.

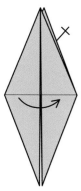

1 Fold through step 4 of the Crane. Move half of the front flap from left to right. Repeat on the back.

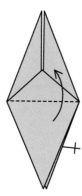

2 Valley-fold up the top flap to the top of the model. Repeat on the back.

3 Valley-fold down until the edge meets the bottom.

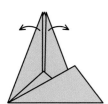

4 Slide the middle points as indicated. Press the bottom when finished.

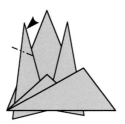

5 Inside-reverse-fold the left point to make the crane's head.

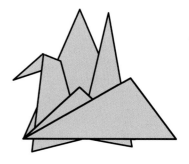

Result

RHINOCEROS

SKILL LEVEL
★ ★ ☆

PAPER SIZE
1½" (3.8cm) for small models

SUGGESTED PROJECTS
This model works well with post earrings because of the opening in the bottom.

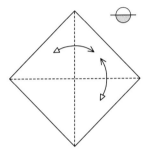

1 With the paper wrong side up, valley-fold and unfold as indicated.

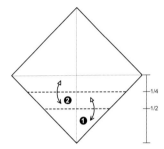

2 Fold and unfold the bottom in half. Then fold and unfold the new upper half.

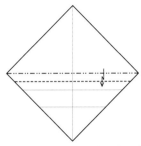

3 Mountain- and valley-fold as indicated.

TIP

This model is flat once you finish folding. However, if you want to use it as a charm with some dimension, keep the lower part of the body open. This will give the rhino a slightly rounded shape.

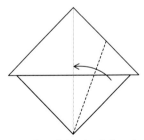

4 Valley-fold the left side until it meets the center.

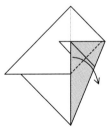

5 Valley-fold down as indicated. Don't fold all the way to the right corner; the fold line should be slightly to the left of the corner.

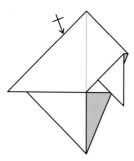

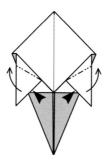

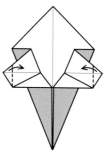

6 Repeat steps 4 and 5 on the left side.

7 Slide the tips to the top (as indicated) until you meet the paper that is stuck.

8 Valley-fold on both sides. These will be the legs. Rotate the model to work on the top.

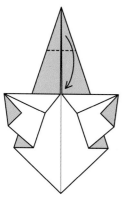

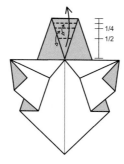

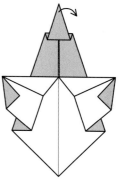

9 Valley-fold down the top triangle in half.

10 Fold and unfold the newly made triangle. Then fold and unfold the top half. Following the newly formed crease, valley-fold up the top half.

11 Move the top triangle to the back without unfolding the last step.

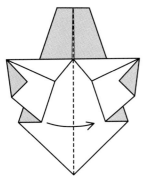

12 Valley-fold the entire model in half and turn it.

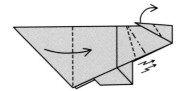

13 Valley-fold to the right to crease the horn. Shape the head with mountain and valley folds on both sides. Valley-fold the left side to begin shaping the tail.

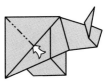

14 Open the triangle, forming a square with a squash fold.

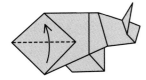

15 Valley-fold up the top layer. This will become the tail in the next step.

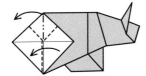

16 Valley-fold the white part to the left to close it while simultaneously incorporating a set of folds to create the tail.

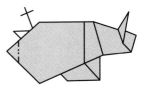

17 Mountain-fold on the left side to shape the model. Repeat behind.

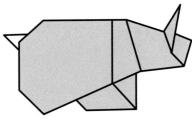

Result

HIPPOPOTAMUS

SKILL LEVEL
★ ★ ☆

PAPER SIZE
1½" (3.8cm) for small models

SUGGESTED PROJECTS
This model works well with post earrings because of the opening in the bottom.

TIP

This hippo is a variation of the Rhinocerus. Open the space below the head to accentuate the hippo's nose and give the hippo a more defined face.

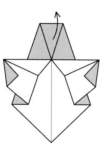

1 Fold steps 1 through 9 of the Rhinoceros. Unfold the top triangle.

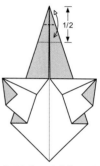

2 Valley-fold and unfold the top half.

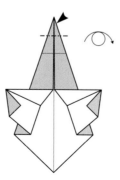

3 Hide the top with the newly formed folds from the previous step. Turn the model over.

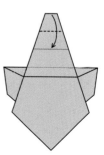

4 Valley-fold down the top half.

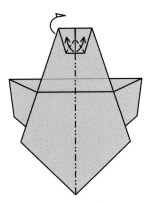

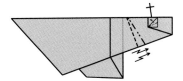

5 Valley-fold at the top as indicated. Mountain-fold the entire model and rotate it.

6 Squash-fold at the nose to give it some shape and show some white paper. Repeat behind. Shape the head with a double set of mountain and valley folds. To shape the tail, follow steps 13 through 17 of the Rhinoceros.

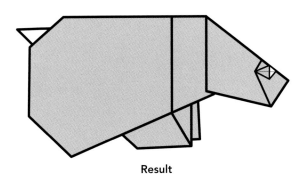

Result

ANGEL

SKILL LEVEL
★ ★ ★

PAPER SIZE
2¾" (7cm) for small models

SUGGESTED PROJECTS
This model works well with projects that need a larger model, such as necklaces, brooches and hairpins.

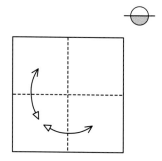

1 With the paper wrong side up, valley-fold and unfold the paper in halves.

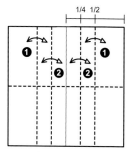

2 Fold and unfold following the order of the numbers.

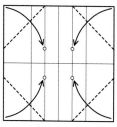

3 Valley-fold the corners as shown.

TIP

This model is flat and thus works well with many of the projects. It is challenging to fold with small paper, however, so I recommend starting with larger paper and working your way down.

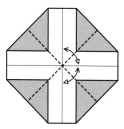

4 Valley-fold and unfold in halves.

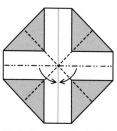

5 Collapse the left and right sides into the center.

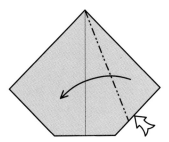

6 Open the right flap, and squash fold it to the left.

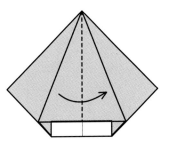

7 Valley-fold to the right.

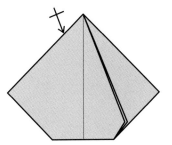

8 Repeat steps 6 and 7 for the left side.

9 After step 8, the model will look like this. Turn it over.

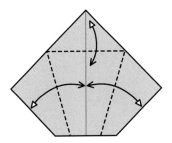

10 Fold and unfold to create creases for step 11.

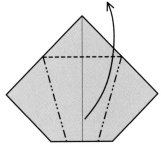

11 Open the bottom and valley-fold to the top, incorporating mountain folds and pushing on the sides.

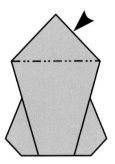

12 Valley-fold down the top.

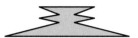

13 Sink all of the top inside. Open the top of the model to do this; you're basically making a mountain fold along the top, and in doing so will hide the top.

14 After step 13, the model will look like this when viewed from the top.

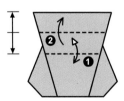

15 Fold and unfold in half. Fold the top half. Be careful when folding as some of the paper on the inside may get stuck.

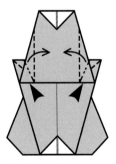

16 Squash-fold to the center where indicated. This will shape the head.

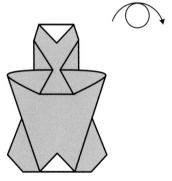

17 After step 16, the model will look like this. Turn it over.

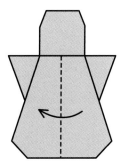 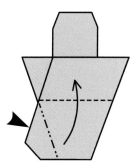 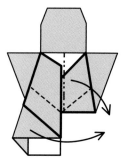

18 Valley-fold the front flap to the left.

19 Open the bottom and valley-fold to the top while pushing the left side to the center.

20 Fold the front flap on the left to the right while shaping the hand with 2 valley folds and a mountain fold at the center.

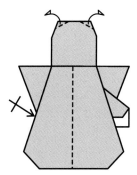

21 Repeat steps 18 through 20 on the left side. Shape the top of the head.

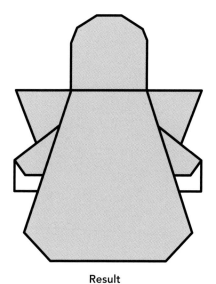

Result

BEAR CUB

SKILL LEVEL
★ ★ ☆

PAPER SIZE
2" (5.1cm) for small models

SUGGESTED PROJECTS
This model works well with dangle earrings, necklaces and bracelets.

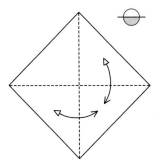

1 With the paper wrong side up, fold and unfold in halves.

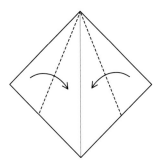

2 Valley-fold both sides to the center.

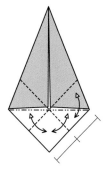

3 Mountain-fold and unfold the bottom triangle. Fold and unfold the bottom in halves.

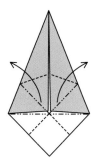

4 Pinch the tips along the mountain folds, and move them up while incorporating the folds from step 3.

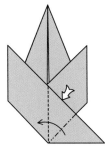

5 Open the bottom a little and squash-fold to create a square at the center. Rotate the model 180°.

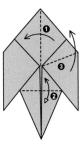

6 Fold the right top flap to the left. Valley-fold and unfold the bottom tip. Valley-fold up the right flap.

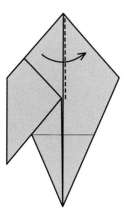

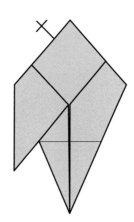

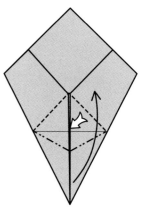

7 Fold the top flap back to the right.

8 Repeat steps 6 and 7 on the left side.

9 Open the middle slightly, and fold up the bottom tip while incorporating a set of mountain and valley folds. Both folds start at step 6's bottom valley fold.

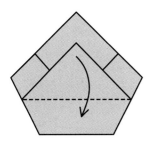

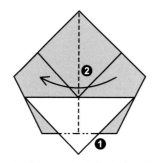

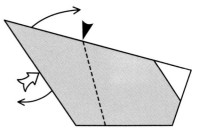

10 Valley-fold down the tip.

11 Mountain-fold behind the bottom tip to create a tail. Valley-fold the entire model in half and rotate 45° counterclockwise.

12 Outside-reverse-fold while taking out some of the paper trapped inside. The trapped paper will shape the head.

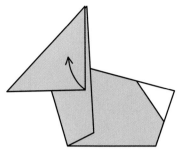

13 Open the head's bottom corner a little (without folding a valley fold).

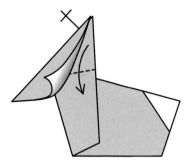

14 Valley-fold down some of the paper trapped inside. Move it until it doesn't let you fold it anymore (without breaking it). Repeat behind.

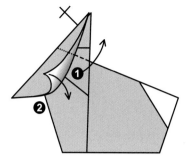

15 Valley-fold up the top that you just folded, then fold down what you did in step 13. Repeat behind. These will be the ears.

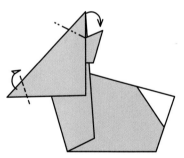

16 Inside-reverse-fold the tip at the top to shape the head. Outside-reverse-fold the top at the left to form the nose.

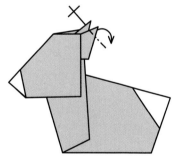

17 Inside-reverse-fold or mountain-fold the tips of the ears.

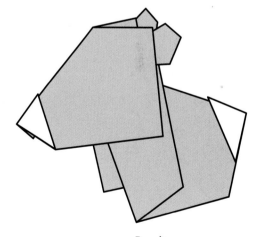

Result

FOX PUP

SKILL LEVEL
★ ★ ★

PAPER SIZE
2" (5.1cm) for small models

SUGGESTED PROJECTS
This model works well with dangle earrings, necklaces and bracelets.

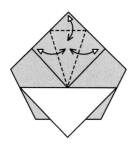

1 Fold steps 1 through 10 of the Bear Cub. Valley-fold the left and right sides to the center. Create a valley fold at the top of the new crease lines.

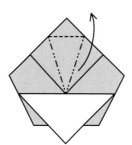

2 Fold up the top flap while pushing in the sides to meet at the center.

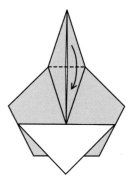

3 Valley-fold down.

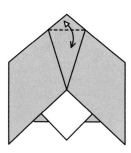

7 Valley-fold and unfold the tip.

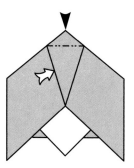

8 Sink the top that you just folded. You'll need to open the top a bit and reach inside to hide the paper at the top.

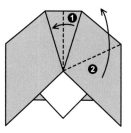

9 Valley-fold the top to the left, then valley-fold up the right flap.

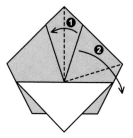

4 Valley-fold the top to the left, then valley-fold down all the way to the right.

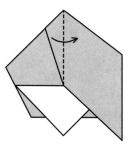

5 Valley-fold back to the right.

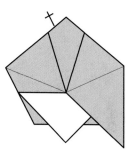

6 Repeat steps 3 and 4 on the left side.

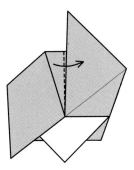

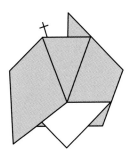

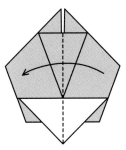

10 Valley-fold the top to the right.

11 Repeat steps 8 and 9 on the left side.

12 Valley-fold the entire model in half, then rotate 45° counterclockwise.

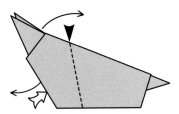

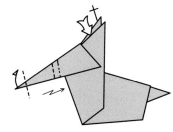

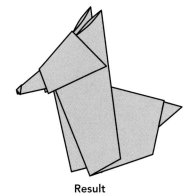

13 Outside-reverse-fold while taking out some of the paper trapped inside. This paper will shape the head.

14 Fold the tip on the left to make a nose. Fold a mountain and valley fold on the left to shape the face. Open both ears slightly.

Result

BRONTOSAURUS

SKILL LEVEL
★ ★ ★

PAPER SIZE
2"–2½" (5.1cm–6.4cm) for small models

SUGGESTED PROJECTS
This model works well with post earrings because of the opening in the bottom.

TIP

This model becomes quite thick when folded. Choose a thin paper, but not so thin that it tears easily.

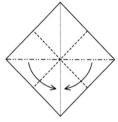

1 With the paper right side up, valley-fold the corners to the center. Turn the paper over.

2 With a set of valley folds dividing the model in halves and a mountain fold down the middle, collapse the right and left corners to the center. Turn the model over. The closed part should be at the top.

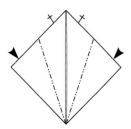

3 Inside-reverse-fold the left and right corners to meet the centerline. Repeat behind.

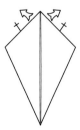

4 Carefully unwrap the paper trapped around both the right and left sides. Repeat behind.

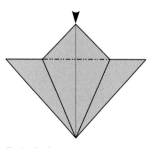

5 Sink the top corner. Open the model slightly to sink the top all the way to the center and flatten.

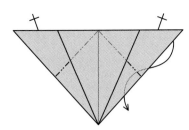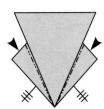

6 Inside-reverse-fold the right and left corners. Notice that some of the paper is trapped inside. It will remain that way. Repeat behind.

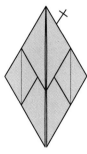

7 Inside-reverse-fold the bottom corners. Repeat 3 times behind for each side.

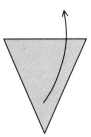

8 Fold and pull the second layer of flaps. The model will not lie flat until step 10.

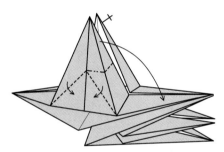

9 After step 8, the model will look like this from the side. On each of the flaps that are not flat, pinch them at the top with a set of valley and mountain folds and flatten the model by folding down what you just pinched. The valley and mountain folds will be created automatically when you pinch the top and fold it down.

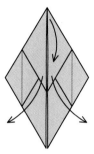

10 Repeat steps 8 and 9 behind.

11 Slide down both middle tips. The model will not lie flat.

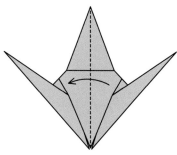

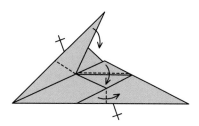

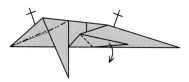

12 Valley-fold the entire model in half. The model will lie flat. Rotate 45° clockwise.

13 Valley-fold down the top to create a leg. Valley-fold the tip in the middle to the right. Repeat behind.

14 Mountain-fold the left top corner to hide some of the paper. Valley-fold down the middle tip to create another leg. Repeat both steps behind.

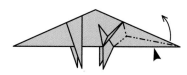

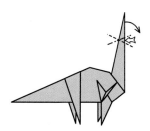

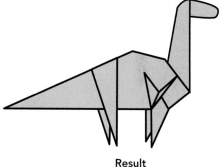

15 Pinch the right side by creating a set of mountain folds on both sides at the same time. This will create the elevated neck.

16 Open the tip of the neck and incorporate a mountain and valley fold to create the head. Round the head by taking out some of the paper from inside.

Result

JEWELRY PROJECTS

The jewelry projects in this book are designed to allow you to use a variety of different origami models in the finished product. You'll find two kinds of projects: jewelry with the origami models glued to a base and jewelry made from origami charms.

For each style, you'll see examples of the various projects you can create. Once you get the hang of the techniques, you can create your own one-of-a-kind pieces.

PREPARING THE MODELS

Once you've finished folding your models, there are a few things you need to do before using the models for jewelry.

APPLY A COATING

You have a choice of several types of coatings to apply to your finished model. The coating will help strengthen the model so it doesn't lose its shape over time. See the Origami Materials section in the first chapter for an overview on the different types of coatings that can be used.

The models may bend out of shape slightly after you apply the coating, especially if you use water. Gluing the models, as described below, can help get them back into shape.

Gluing the wing in place

GLUE THE MODELS

Gluing your models makes them more secure and can anchor some of the folds for a cleaner, more precise model. You can also use glue to give some dimension to your pieces, rounding out the arms of the Japanese Man, for example, or the ears of the Fox Pup.

Flat models

When gluing flat models, think about your finished jewelry piece. Don't accidentally glue an opening shut that you need open to create your piece. Use a small amount of glue. A toothpick can help you get a just a dab of glue in hard-to-reach places.

Finished model: all the openings have been glued shut

Three-dimensional models

It's possible to add dimension to your models with the help of glue. You can bend and glue the arms of the Japanese Man, shape the ears of the Fox Pup or round the nose of the Hippopotamus. Look for places on the model where you can glue at different angles.

Apply the glue sparingly. You don't want to cover the entire model in glue, just the places where the papers meet. Once you've created some dimension, you'll want to glue down the other areas of the model that need securing.

Bending origami models

Sometimes something as simple as bending part of an opening can give the model dimension and movement. The Elephant, Fox and Sitting Dog all benefit from this technique. Apply glue to half of the opening. Let the glue dry, then gently pull open the unglued portion.

Apply the coating to your model after you've finished bending it. Some of the coatings will make it hard to move the paper, so it's better to shape your model before you apply the coating.

Gluing the Japanese Man's arm to give dimension

Gluing the base of the Elephant's ears, then bending the tops of the ears to add shape

ATTACHED ORIGAMI MODEL JEWELRY

The simplest way to create stylish jewelry from your origami models is to glue the model directly to the jewelry, whether it's a necklace chain, ring, headband or something else. I'll show you a few different methods for creating the jewelry and examples of the different projects you can make using these techniques.

demonstration | ATTACHING MODELS

DOUBLE-SIDED METHOD

Glue two origami models back to back (one will need to be the mirror image of the other) over a chain or cord to create a bracelet or necklace that looks as good from the front as it does from the back.

MATERIALS LIST

2 flat origami models (one the mirror image of the other)

Finished bracelet (either cord or chain)

Glue

1 Apply glue to the wrong side of each of the origami models.

2 Position one of the models on the bracelet, then align the second model behind the first, sandwiching the bracelet cord between the two models. Let the glue dry completely.

SINGLE-SIDED METHOD

Even simpler than the double-sided method, this method uses a matching piece of paper on the back side of the origami model to wrap around the jewelry, whether it's a necklace, headband or ring. This method works best if the origami model is relatively flat.

MATERIALS LIST

1 flat origami model

Matching paper

Finished necklace (either cord or chain)

Scissors

Glue

1 Carefully cut a piece of paper into the shape of your model.

2 Apply glue to the wrong side of the paper and place the chain on top of the glue where you want your model to be.

3 Layer the origami model on top of the paper, sandwiching the chain in between. Let the glue dry completely. To make the model more secure, glue on multiple layers of paper on the back side.

DIRECT METHOD

Because the earring post is attached directly through the origami model, those that have openings in the bottom, such as the Sitting Dog, Hippopotamus, Rhinocerus, Fox Pup and Stocking, work best.

MATERIALS LIST

Pair of origami models with openings

Earring posts

Sharp needle

Glue

1 Poke a hole on the back side of the origami model where the earring post will come through. The hole should be somewhat centered on the model and should leave enough room to hide the metal back of the earring post behind the model.

2 Slide the earring post through the hole and add a small amount of glue to the opening of the model. Gently squeeze the opening shut so that the glue adheres. Let the glue dry.

3 Once the glue is dry, you can slide on the earring back. Repeat with the other origami model.

demonstration | POST EARRINGS

INDIRECT METHOD

Use this method for flat origami models or those that don't have an opening suitable for hiding the earring post. Try the Sailboat, Flat Crane, Shirt, Christmas Tree, Fractal Rose and Heart.

MATERIALS LIST

Pair of flat origami models

Earring posts

Sharp needle

Glue

Scissors

Piece of paper (same color/pattern as origami models)

1 Cut a piece of paper to match the shape of your origami model. Cut 4 to 6 of these shapes.

2 Poke a hole in the paper where the earring post will go through. The hole should be roughly in the center of the paper.

3 Slide the earring post through the hole, making sure that the metal blank is on the wrong side of the paper.

4 Cover the wrong side of the paper with glue.

5 Glue the paper to the wrong side of your model. To make the earring more secure, add another piece of paper to the earring, following steps 2–4.

6 Once the glue is dry, slide on the earring back. Repeat to make the other earring.

CHARM JEWELRY

You can use origami charms to make simple and elegant necklaces and bracelets. Follow the tutorials for turning your origami models into charms, then use either the loose charm method or the anchored charm method to turn the charms into jewelry.

demonstration | MAKING CHARMS

Turning your origami models into charms is one of the building blocks for jewelry making in this book. By simply stringing the charms onto a cord, you can easily make necklaces and bracelets. Many of the jewelry projects in this book will refer back to the three techniques explained in this section, so flag these pages!

DIRECT METHOD
This method attaches a metal eye pin directly to the origami figure by running the wire through the figure and pinching the wire tight.

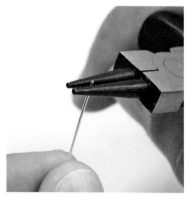

1 Cut a small amount of wire or trim an eye pin to size. The length of wire needed will depend on your finished project. If you plan on adding beads, cut it a little longer. I will be adding beads in this demo, so I cut my wire about 1½" (4cm).

2 If you're using wire, you'll need to create an eye at the end of your wire. Grab the tip of the wire with the round-nose pliers. If you need a small eye, grab the wire with the very tip of the pliers. Grab the wire further back on the pliers for a larger eye.

MATERIALS LIST

Flat or 3-D origami model, such as the traditional Crane, Fox Pup, Hippopotamus, Elephant or Samurai Helmet

22-gauge wire in color of your choice, or an eye pin or a flat head pin

Sharp needle

Chain-nose pliers

Round-nose pliers

Flush cutters

Beads (optional)

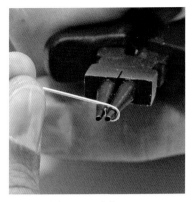 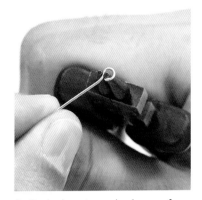 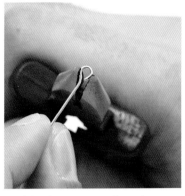

3 Bend the tip of the wire around the pliers.

4 Grab the pin at the base of the loop you just created and bend it back away from the loop so that the loop is centered over the wire.

5 If the loop is not closed, gently close it with your chain-nose pliers. You have made an eye pin.

  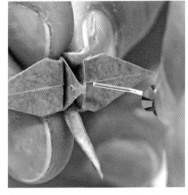

6 Using a sharp needle, poke a hole through your origami model where the eye pin will be inserted. Make sure the hole isn't too close to the edge of the model or it may eventually tear.

7 If you're using beads, slide them onto the eye pin now.

8 Slide the straight end of the eye pin through the origami model.

9 Using your fingers or pliers, gently bend the wire end up. If you'd like your eye pin shorter, you can pull through a longer tail and trim it. Be careful not to cut your model.

10 With the round-nose pliers, create a small hook in the wire. This hook will wrap around the origami figure, pinching it and holding it in place.

11 Holding the top of the eye pin in one hand, squeeze the wire on both sides of the model with your pliers so that the model is secure. The short end of the wire should stop at the top of the model; carefully trim it if necessary.

12 Use your chain-nose pliers to grasp the eye pin loop and gently twist to desired position..

| # MAKING CHARMS

INDIRECT METHOD 1

This method also requires you to pinch an eye pin around paper, but the paper is separate from the origami model and glued on after the fact. This technique is perfect for flat models that need a more subtle attachment. I recommend this method for the Christmas Tree, Shirt, Stocking, Angel, Elephant and others.

MATERIALS LIST

Flat origami model, such as the Christmas Tree, Shirt, Stocking or Angel

Scrap of paper (preferably the paper you used for the model)

22-gauge wire in a color of your choice, or an eye pin or a flat head pin

Sharp needle

Chain-nose pliers

Round-nose pliers

Flush cutters

Scissors

Glue

Beads (optional)

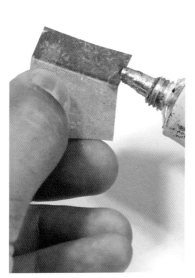

1 Starting with a piece of paper roughly the size of the paper used to fold the model, fold 1 edge of the paper to the middle. Glue the fold in place.

2 Once the glue has dried, cut off the excess paper (the part that isn't doubled).

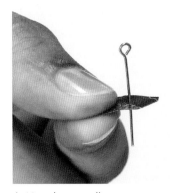

3 Cut the double paper into a shape that roughly matches the outline of your origami model.

4 Use the needle to create a hole in the doubled paper for the eye pin. Slide the eye pin through the hole. Follow steps 1 through 5 of the direct method to make your own eye pin.

5 Using your fingers or the chain-nose pliers, bend the wire at a 45-degree angle. Make sure the eye of the pin is oriented so that your charm hangs the way you want it to on your finished piece.

6 Trim the wire so that the end doesn't extend past the doubled paper. Use the chain-nose pliers to pinch the wire tightly around the paper.

7 Add a small amount of glue to the back of the doubled paper (the side with the short end of the eye pin).

8 Press the doubled paper to the back of your origami model and let it dry.

9 From the paper you trimmed off in the second step, cut a backing piece that's roughly the shape of the origami figure.

10 Glue the backing piece over the back of your figure, sandwiching the eye pin between the layers.

MAKING THE FRONT AND BACK THE SAME

Though gluing a paper backing to your project will give you a neatly finished back side, there are times when you might want both sides of your charm to look the same. If you're making a pair of dangle earrings, for example, either side may face the front at times. In these cases, you can take the extra step of gluing a second completed model to your paper backing. Depending on your model, you may need to fold the backing model in reverse so that you have a mirror image of the piece.

INDIRECT METHOD 2

This method is similar to Indirect Method 1, but the paper with the eye pin is hidden within the folds of the model. For that reason, 3-D models work best, especially ones that don't have a right or wrong side.

MATERIALS LIST

3-D origami model, such as the Fox Pup, Rhinocerus, Hippopotamus, Samurai Helmet or Sitting Dog

Piece of paper (preferably the paper you used for the model)

22-gauge wire in a color of your choice or a flat head pin

Sharp needle

Chain-nose pliers

Round-nose pliers

Flush cutters

Scissors

Glue

Beads (optional)

1 Fold the paper in half and glue the 2 sides together. The paper doesn't need to match your origami model because it will be hidden inside the model. Let the glue dry.

2 Use the needle to create a small hole in the paper. This is where you will place the flat head pin.

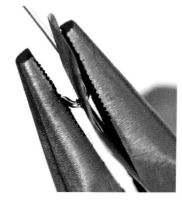

3 Insert a length of wire through the hole in the paper.If you are using a flat head pin, cut the flat end off the pin using the flush cutters

4 With the round-nose pliers, grab the wire at the very tip. Bend the wire to create a semicircle.

5 With the chain-nose pliers, pinch flat the semicircle you just made. The flat end of the circle will bite into the paper, making the connection more secure.

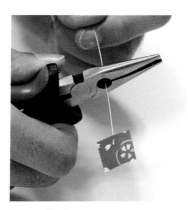

6 Use flush cutters to trim excess wire.

7 Trim the double paper so that it is small enough to fit inside the orgami model without showing. For the Fox Pup (shown), the paper will be inserted right in the middle of the model, with the wire coming out of the top.

8 Make a hole in the origami model with the needle. This is where you will insert the wire and paper. Try to keep the hole in the center of the model to keep it balanced.

9 Add glue to both sides of the paper to be inserted.

10 Thread the wire through the bottom of the model, and pull it through the hole in the top. Continue threading it through until the paper with the glue is completely inside the model.

11 Press together both sides of the model to help the glue adhere. If any paper hangs out of the model, carefully trim it.

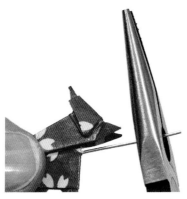

12 If you plan on adding beads to your charm, this is the time to add them. Make sure you leave enough wire to create an eye pin. Double-check the length of your wire and trim it, if necessary.

13 Grab the end of the wire with the round-nose pliers. Consider how large of an opening your finished project requires: grabbing the wire near the tip of the pliers will make a small circle; grabbing the wire farther down will create a larger circle.

14 Bend the wire around the round-nose pliers, creating a circle. The loop will be to the side of the wire.

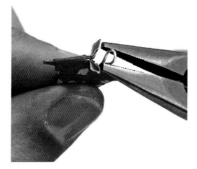

15 Grab the wire at the base of the circle and bend it gently so that the circle is directly on top of the wire.

16 Close the circle by gently squeezing it with the chain-nose pliers.

LOOSE CHARM METHOD

The loose charm method is endlessly adaptable. Simply string your charms on a cord or chain that's the appropriate length for a necklace or bracelet. Then add beads (if desired) and add a clasp. Simple!

MATERIALS LIST

Origami charm (as many as you want)

Beads (optional)

Leather cord

2 end caps, 1 with lobster clasp attached

Glue, such as E6000

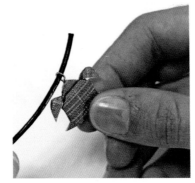

1 Determine the desired length of your bracelet or necklace and trim the cord to that length. If you're unsure of the length, 7½"–8" (19.1cm–20.3cm) is a standard bracelet length and 12"–18" (30.5–45.7cm) is standard for necklaces.

2 Thread the charm onto the cord. If you're using multiple charms or beads, add them now.

CORD THICKNESS

Choose your cord for this project before you make your charms. You'll need to make sure the eye of the charm is large enough to fit around the cord.

Also, pay attention to the size of the end caps you buy. They should fit snugly over the leather cord.

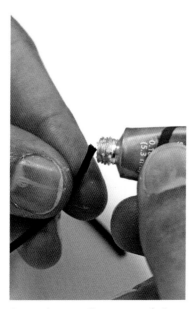

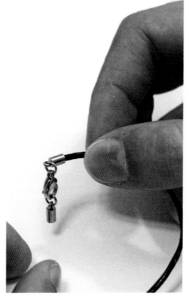

3 Apply a small amount of glue to each end of the cord.

4 Slide the end caps over the cord ends. If any excess glue comes out of the caps, wipe it away.

5 Let the glue dry completely before you wear your new piece.

ADDING CHARMS TO JEWELRY

POSITIONED CHARM METHOD

The positioned charm method works best with a chain. Attach the eye pin of your charm directly through a link in the chain to anchor it. The project shown here uses three butterfly charms with the center charm made from a larger square of paper.

MATERIALS LIST

3 flat origami charms (or as many as desired)

Chain-nose pliers

Round-nose pliers

Chain in desired length

Lobster clasp

2 jump rings

1 Open a jump ring using both pairs of pliers. Slide the lobster clasp onto the jump ring and close the jump ring.

2 Add a jump ring to the other end of the chain.

OPENING A JUMP RING

Always open jump rings by twisting the sides away from each other, rather than pulling straight back; if you pull straight back, you'll lose the circular shape of the jump ring.

3 Find the center of the chain. You can do this by measuring the chain or simply folding the chain in half.

4 Using your chain-nose pliers, open the eye pin on your center charm.

5 Thread the eye pin through the center link of your chain.

6 Use the chain-nose pliers to close the eye pin on the center charm.

7 Determine the position for the remaining charms, if you will be adding more. To make sure the charms are equal distances from the center charm, count the number of chain links on each side.

8 Use the chain-nose pliers to open the eye pin on one of the remaining charms and thread it through the chain. Close the eye pin and repeat with the remaining charm.

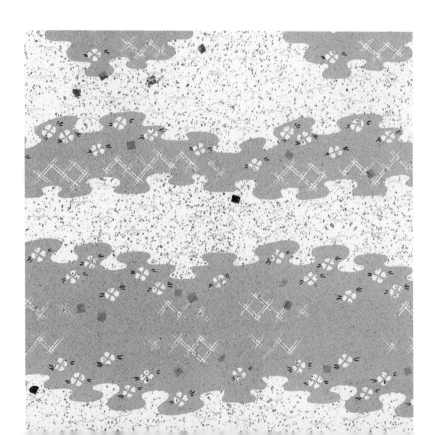

1 flat origami model

Matching paper

Blank ring base

Scissors

Metal glue, such as J-B Weld

Paper glue

RING

The ring uses the single-side method for attaching a model to the blank ring base. I recommend using two types of glue for this project: one meant for adhering paper to metal and one for adhering paper to paper. Use the metal/paper glue for gluing your model directly to the ring base, and use the paper glue to glue the paper backing to the model.

TRIM THE PAPER BACKING

If you're attaching your model to a ring base, pin, headband or something with some thickness to it, you may need to cut your paper backing with a little extra length to wrap around the object. You can always trim any excess paper away once the glue has dried.

BROOCH

The single-sided method works best for the brooch, as do origami models with flat backs. Again, you'll want to use two types of glue, one to glue the model directly onto the flat part of the brooch and another for gluing the paper backing in place.

MATERIALS LIST

1 flat origami model

Matching paper

Blank pin or brooch base

Scissors

Metal glue, such as J-B Weld

Paper glue

HEADBAND

Use the single-sided method to attach flat origami models to a headband. Glue at least two pieces of paper on the back of the origami model to attach it securely to the headband base.

DOUBLE NECKLACE

The Fractal Rose necklace shown here uses the double-sided method but can be made just as easily with the single-sided method. Fold the center Fractal Rose using a slightly larger piece of paper to give your necklace added visual interest.

MATERIALS LIST

5 flat origami models (10 models for the double-model method)

Matching paper (for single-model method)

Necklace

Scissors

Glue

FOLD THE MIRROR IMAGE

If you're making the double-model method, you may need to fold the mirror image of your model to glue to the back side. For symmetrical models such as the Fractal Rose, you don't need to worry about folding the mirror image.

MATERIALS LIST

Flat origami model

Hairpin with metal disc

Metal glue, such as J-B Weld

HAIRPINS

Turning your origami models into hairpins is very simple. Glue the flat back of an origami model directly to the blank base of the hairpin and let it dry. Look for hair pins that come with a blank metal disc attached so that you can glue your origami model to the metal disc. Be sure to use a metal glue for adhering the paper to the metal disc of the hairpin.

POST EARRINGS

Post earrings are simple and stylish. Depending on the origami model you choose, you'll either insert the earring posts directly through the model (direct method) or attach the post to a piece of paper first, then glue it to the model (indirect method).

MATERIALS LIST

Pair of flat origami models

Earring posts

Sharp needle

Glue

Scissors

Piece of paper (same color/pattern as origami models)

CHARM BRACELET

Turn your favorite models into charms, and attach them to jump rings. Then, simply close the jump ring around the premade bracelet. If your premade bracelet has beads, evenly space the charms between the beads.

SINGLE CHARM NECKLACE

Using either the loose charm or positioned charm method, you can easily create a statement piece by adding your favorite model to a necklace chain or cord. The dinosaur shown here was attached using the loose charm method. Both 3-D and flat models work well for this type of necklace.

MATERIALS LIST

Origami charm

Necklace chain with clasp

Chain-nose pliers

MATERIALS LIST

3 origami charms

Necklace chain with clasp

Chain-nose pliers

MULTIPLE CHARM NECKLACE

Use the positioned charm method to add multiple charms to a necklace chain. In the sample below, I folded the center butterfly from a slightly larger paper. Flat charms work best for this necklace. Experiment with different combinations: try two Butterflies on either side of a Fractal Rose or a Stocking with Christmas Trees for a holiday themed variation.

DANGLE EARRINGS

Use any of the techniques from the charm section to turn a pair of your origami creations into earrings. Add beads to the charms to make your earrings even more special. Both 3-D and flat models work well for these earrings. Simply twist open the loop end of the fishhook earrings, slide on your charm and close the loop.

MATERIALS LIST

Pair of origami charms

Pair of fishhook earrings

Chain-nose pliers

EARRING TIPS

Keep these tips in mind when you're making earrings:

- Depending on the orgami model you choose, you may want to fold one of the models as a mirror image of the other.
- When making the charms, pay attention to which direction your eye hook is facing. For fishhooks, make the charm with the eye of the pin parallel to the origami model.

INDEX

a content + ecommerce company

www.fwcommunity.com

20   19   18   17   16   5   4   3   2   1

DISTRIBUTED IN CANADA BY FRASER DIRECT
100 Armstrong Avenue
Georgetown, ON, Canada L7G 5S4
Tel: (905) 877-4411

DISTRIBUTED IN THE U.K. AND EUROPE BY F&W MEDIA INTERNATIONAL
Brunel House, Newton Abbot, Devon, TQ12 4PU, England
Tel: (+44) 1626 323200; Fax: (+44) 1626 323319
Email: enquiries@fwmedia.com

DISTRIBUTED IN AUSTRALIA BY CAPRICORN LINK
P.O. Box 704, S. Windsor NSW, 2756 Australia
Tel: (02) 4560 1600; Fax: (02) 4577 5288
Email: books@capricornlink.com.au

SRN: T6849
ISBN-13: 978-1-4402-4423-0

Edited by Stephanie White
Designed by Michelle Thompson
Production coordinated by Jennifer Bass
Beauty photography by OMS
Step-by-step photography by José Orlando Sued
Illustrations by Juan Laboy

DEDICATION

I dedicate this book to my family, who is always there when I need them.

ABOUT THE AUTHOR

Julián Laboy-Rodríguez started folding over a decade ago, as a simple diversion between college classes. He found both a diversion and a new passion. He sells his origami jewelry and other creations in his Etsy store, PaperEdge. Julián lives in Puerto Rico and is currently working on his second M.A. in Psychology.

ACKNOWLEDGMENTS

First of all, thanks to F+W. A big thank you goes to Amelia Johanson for believing in my work; to Stephanie White for editing and for always being available; and to everyone at F+W who contributed in some way.

Second, thanks to my team. I am referring to Juan Laboy, my father, for creating all of the great and detailed origami diagrams; José Orlando Sued, my photographer, for the beautiful step-by-step photos; and Roberto Vázquez for his help in proof editing the origami diagrams. Thank you all for your hard work.

Lastly, thanks to everyone who has seen my work and enjoyed it. That includes customers, family, significant other and friends. I continue my work thanks to your support, comments and love.

MORE BOOKS TO KEEP YOU FOLDING!

ORIGAMI WORLD
40 Fun Paper-Folding Projects
by Didier Boursin
$16.99; ISBN: 978-1-4403-0918-2

The ultimate origami starter book! Inside *Origami World,* readers will find everything they need to create with origami fun. For those new to the world of folding, basic origami techniques are provided. Next comes the projects: 40 fun and fabulous projects from planes that fly to decorative animals and boxes and toys to be used on any occasion—all with clearly illustrated instructions.

ANIMALS IN ORIGAMI
Over 35 Amazing Paper Animals
by Didier Boursin
$16.99; ISBN: 978-1-4463-0231-6

Learn the art of paper folding with over 35 fun animal models. Create your favorite pets, birds and wildlife, from bunnies and butterflies to elephants and monkeys. With easy to follow step-by-step instructions and practical diagrams, even novice folders will quickly master these techniques. Start with the simpler projects to learn the basics, and then have a go at the more challenging designs!